For

Tired - Frustrated - Angry - Morose

Teachers

---

52 Quotes
For daily strength and guidance.
Included are helpful annotations…and a bit of humor!

Nicholas Landers

InlandMedia
Real.Creative.Fun.

Dedicated to Naomi

Contents.

Foreword.

When Nick sent me a copy of this book, I didn't know what I was holding. But because it was *him*, I knew it had to be something good. As an award-winning public speaker of 10 years, focusing on the areas of self-esteem ("Am I Too Sexy?") and mental health, I've seen a lot in the self-development space, and I'm here to tell you this book incredibly refreshing. It leads from the heart and showcases not only a passion for teaching, but also a path towards bolstering a teacher's dignity. His ability to motivate really shines with lines such as "minor aspirations do not generate the energy to persevere," and "Living, playing, and working in the world allows you to *read* others and to *read* your own story." I frequently caught myself thinking *"he's narrowed his audience too finely..."* because this information easily extends beyond the classroom. What you have here is a book founded on principles.

This book's size is also conducive for referencing, whether you're having a rough day and need an uplifting reminder, you're looking for something to share with a fellow coworker, or you just want to share some wise words of wisdom with students.

If your personal life is in disarray, Nick explains how to overcome adversity at home while remaining professional at work; if you're on the verge of quitting the profession, he gently reminds you of your hidden worth. Conversely, if you're a celebrated educator seeking new heights, he articulates a path towards the stars.

Stan Pearson II, MBA

Award-Winning Speaker and Motivational Comedian

Breathe Diversity, LLC

Preface.

Thank you so much for purchasing this book. It's funny, this book developed by accident—or maybe not. I want to briefly take you through how this book came about and its ultimate purpose. It is my greatest hope that by sharing the insights I've gained along the way, my real-life experiences and trials will empower and enlighten fellow teachers throughout what can be a tumultuous school year. I will then close with a few acknowledgments. Okay, let's begin!

Last year, March 2018, I suffered a mild—but serious to me—panic attack. It was the first time I'd felt anything like that. My chest was tight and my breaths were shallow...and it happened while I was at work! As I was walking around the classroom, monitoring student engagement and assisting others, I nearly stumbled because my head suddenly grew unbearably light and I lost some feeling in my legs. Placing my hands on a student's desk nearby, startling her, she looked up at me and asked, "Mr. Landers, are you okay?" I was terrified, and felt as if I might faint. I didn't even know how people fainted but I thought that I might. In fact, until last year I thought most people just faked it. Looking down at her, I smiled and said, "I'm good, but thanks for checking on me." I made one more lap around the room and then sat down at my desk, gawking at the time on my wrist-I had 30 more minutes until the bell sounded, signaling the end of the day. The worst part? I feared I wouldn't make it another three.

Honest to God, I'd never felt time move so slowly. It made me furious. I can laugh about it now but it was not funny then. The sweep moved as if it were cutting through syrup, and the minute hand just stood there like a sturdy maple in the dead of winter. Dread and sweat covered my face as I cupped my head, elbows resting on the desk, contemplating my imminent death. Naturally, I began to assess- and reassess-my life and take inventory of my biggest accomplishments...and more importantly, dreams yet realized. Thoughts like I'm too young to go out like this and I should've quit a long time ago filled my brain.-

Thoughts like those kept me busy until the bell rang. I gathered my belongings and headed to the door, nearly at the same time as the children, as if I'd been dismissed, too. I tried to sneak out of the building's side door-and was almost successful-until I saw the principal guarding the door, arms folded. Technically, I couldn't clock out until 3:45...and it was only 3:12. I wanted to scream; I wanted to cry; I wanted to give her a piece of my mind. Instead, I coolly turned the corner and hid in an occupied classroom. I sat there until the coast was clear, ashamed and angry on the inside but making conversation on the outside. I don't recall any of the conversations that followed, just the sound of my car rumbling, sitting in the driver's seat nervous as hell because I was in no state to drive.

Thirty minutes later, free from the madness of Atlanta traffic (which wasn't that bad), I was anxiously waiting to be called back to the doctor. I'd never been so excited to visit Urgent Care in my life!

"Mr. Landers, you can follow me," said a pleasant, middle-aged woman.

I leaped from my chair, trailing behind until we met an open doorway. I sat down on the papered recliner and was completely vulnerable. I was ready to throw my hands up, grovel, or fully disrobe for a complete check-up (which wasn't necessary). The nurse took the standard vitals and then disappeared. Moments later, the doctor entered and simply asked me what was going on, conducted a few more tests...and then I was back in the waiting area.

I stared out of a tiny window, envying the few pedestrians below. Why me? That's all I could think. How could someone who helped children and sacrificed so much leave the planet so soon? In a way, I was resigned to my fate...on the other hand, I was prepared to fight.

"Mr. Landers," the doctor called. Relief swathed my bosom. "I'm recommending you to the emergency room. I've already made the call. Please visit this hospital." The news felt fatal, like I'd been involved in a really bad car wreck.

"Are you okay to drive, sir? I can arrange transport."

I lifted my head high and took the small paper in his hands. And then I walked downstairs and back to my car, inputting the address in my GPS. I drove off with tears welling up in my eyes.

I arrived at Emory University Hospital Midtown around 7:30pm. I'd seldom been to a hospital, much less for myself. I followed the signs to the ER and took a number. Nearly every seat was taken. Long faces, tears, shakes, and fatigue painted the scene. This was it- this was where all of my choices had taken me-31 years old and experiencing stroke-like symptoms. I didn't know who to call. I couldn't worry my parents, and I wondered if any of my friends cared, truly cared. My phone's battery life was alarmingly low, and I didn't know how I would manage, unsure how long the wait would be.

I ended up waiting three hours. My left arm had gone numb, and my neck was so tight I could barely turn my head. In the interim, I had borrowed an Android charger, typed my last will and testament, and spoken with my father- the only one I believed was capable of handling the news. I was morose. I was defeated. I was in the throes of madness.

When my name was called, I sauntered back and dryly answered their questions. I took an EKG, X-ray, and blood test...and, once again, returned to a waiting room.

Around 30 minutes later I was called back. A young doctor had a file in his hand and a smile on his face. For the first time all night I felt hopeful.

"Mr. Landers, we didn't find anything. Everything looks to be normal."

Panic surged involuntarily.

"Oh no, there's definitely something wrong. Trust me. Test me again."

"Tell me what you're feeling."

I told him.

"Sounds to me like you may have been, and still might be, dehydrated."

"I'm positive it's not dehydration."

"Well, sir, I can't keep you here."

"No, you have to!"

"I'm sorry but I have to discharge you."

I didn't know what to say. I was relieved, and yet I thought I might die in my sleep. I walked out with a pyrrhic victory.

Long story short, I later discovered it had been a panic attack and that...

Teaching had put me in the hospital.

No doubt teaching is stressful; it's one of the most stressful careers in the United States—Google it. Somewhere along the way, I'd begun bottling everything up and not dealing with my negative emotions. There was a student who could single-handedly ruin an entire lesson; there were impossible test scores to achieve; thieves who helped themselves to loose articles- including the teacher's. There were UFC-level fights in the hallways, disabilities to contend with both in the classroom (behaviorally) and in lesson planning (academically). There were unending professional development workshops that often seemed pointless; endless initiatives coming down from the state, initiatives that felt like anyone but an educator had drawn them up. There were parents to call, parents to placate, parents to educate on...parenting. And before that fateful day in the ER, I figured that was my job-that I was just supposed to take it. After all, that's what teachers are encouraged to do: make the best of challenging situations, limited resources, and low salaries.

But that's wrong.

I needed a painful reminder.

What was it?

I'm a person.

Teachers aren't perfect people, but we're expected to be. We're expected to be role models, even-tempered in all manner of precarious situations, and soundboards for those who are finding themselves; never mind the fact that we may still be in the process of finding ourselves- who we want to be as a person, educator, husband or wife, son or daughter. I think I was tired of pretending like I always had the right answer, and that I could do everything alone.

That's when it struck me! I should create a resource to help empower, inspire, and educate teachers who are dangerously close to losing themselves for the greater good.

That's how this book came about, only, one year later :)

When it came to penning this, I wasn't sure how I'd relate my message. As I was already in the process of writing a novel, I didn't want to start another. I needed something shorter. All sorts of ideas came to mind- novellas, pamphlets, podcasts, Instagram series, etc., but none of those 'worked.' I wanted a book rooted in timely principles. To that end, I thought of religious texts and sagacious philosophers; and after a day at the pool, I decided a small book of quotes would be enough. So I collected 52 quotes- one for each week- and formatted them in a Word document. Finished! Or so I thought. The book didn't express how teachers were supposed to use them. I mean, sure, quotes are intuitive enough but I wanted something practical. I needed teachers to know that I understand them. So I annotated them with my own sort of philosophy developed over my last 10 years of teaching. I thought I was a good person for that.

I've taught on three continents: Japan, Germany, and the U.S. Adapted content/instruction to educational standards like Common Core and International Baccalaureate. I've worn many hats like Reading Specialist, assistant language teacher, ELA teacher, and educational consultant. Won an international tournament as head basketball coach, and leveraged my college track and field career into an assistant coach position in two countries. I've sponsored art, English, mentoring, and debate clubs. Been a dorm parent to 31 boys at a boarding school. I mean, I've taught (and lived) at a boarding school! I've been to 30+ countries and can speak enough of a few languages to get around with little difficulty.

I hope you will find something of value inside these pages; something enriching and bracing; something wonderful.

❊❊

Acknowledgments.

A big thank you to my editor, Mrs. Sarina Cornthwaite, for her hard work, attention to detail, timeliness and fruitful insights.

The high school teachers responsible for instilling in me a love for learning and a commitment to academic and athletic excellence: Dr. Jimmy Stokes, Mr. Timothy Kemp, Mr. Brad Williford, Mr. Marvin Oliver, Ms. Samantha Purcell, Dr. Carole Hicks, Mr. Ronnie Coleman, and Mrs. Linda Head.

My Monroe Area High School family: Ms. Kim Brown, Mrs. Pam Bell, Ms. Ruby Lawson, Dr. Kimberly Brown, Dr. Rita Dickinson, Ms. Amanda Foley, Mrs. Subrina Doty, Ms. Nicole Richards, Ms. Sarah Sapinski, Ms. Sarah Johnson, Ms. Ivy Corder, Mr. Nick Helfrick, The Mansour family, Mr. Jeremiah Bundrage, Ms. Blair Inabinet, and Ms. Meredith Farmer.

My Schule Schloss Salem family: Herr Bert Sinner, Frau Heidi Sinner, Mr. Jason Corbet, Ms. Karen Napoli, the Ellen family, Mr. Mario Sagastume, and Herr Eugen Balzer.

Miller Grove, stand up! - Dr. Latashia Searcy, Mrs. Arnise Owens, Mr. Randel Johnnicon, Ms. Morgan House, Mr. Tyron Roberts, Mr. Sean Hill, Ms. Karen Banks, Ms. Latasha Farmer, Mr. Matthew Priester, Mr. Adrian Warden, Ms. Yvette White, Dr. Sujuan Graham, CHEF Keio Gayden, Ms. Nina Jenkins, Mr. Eric Keddo, Ms. Amy Larrimore, Ms. Michelle Watkins, and Mr. Lavontai Wynn.

My Interac family: Kato sensei, Suzuki sensei, Sato sensei, Chiba sensei, Ono sensei, Takahashi sensei, Sakai sensei, Mr. Dave Yang, Ms. Patricia Lefevre, Ms. Cindy Grey, Ms. Keri Beri, Siri, and Ms. Ashley Cox.

To my friends—too many of you to list! Samuel Wright Jr., Stan Pearson II, Nick Crawford, Tristian Smith, Jarmel Calvin, Mack Hardwick, Sierra Kulas, Brandon Edwards, Brandon Johnson, Virgil Pearson, Bryan Ramey, Mandrell Ramey, Kayla McCurry, Michael Koch, Kenyatta Taliaferro, Miriam Delfino, Natalia

Krslovic, John Wright, Charles Barnwell, Dr. Whitney Ginder, Dr. Khalilah Robinson-Johnson, Brandon Porter, Ryan Gaus, Adrian Edwards, Christopher Hewitt, Dwight Bush, and Carl Burkins... for always believing in me, protecting me, and helping me find a way forward. You are celebrated.

A special thank you to the Landers family for setting a sturdy foundation, one rooted in faith, character, and service. You've been instrumental in forging me into who I am today, and I'm sincerely appreciative of your sacrifices and dedication. Shout-out to my sister, Tandra, who has been a little bit of everything to me — from music critic to racing partner. You the best, mane :) And can't forget my nephew CJ3! What a fun-loving and curious kid.

Fifty-two **Quotes.**

F.O.R. SERIES
FACING OBSTACLES REALISTICALLY

TEACHER EDITION

1.

IN the hour of adversity be not without hope, for crystal rain falls from black clouds.

Nizāmī.

Translation - Grades are due, kids are fighting, parents are emailing, your neighbor needs coverage, and professional development seminars are underway. What do you do? Keep your head up because something good will come of it eventually... eventually.

The education system may appear antiquated and the students may appear despondent. Nevertheless, you should focus on what you can change. Some of your favorite and most successful students have often been the ones who started out a little rough. Instead of sharp words, greet them with a smile or a hug. There may come a time when you require a particular administrator, parent, or student to help you along—sports banquets, grading, coverage, etc. The quote says "'hour' of adversity," so keep in mind that whatever is bothering you will pass. My advice: let it pass and extract the lesson it is offering.

2.

I asked an experienced elder who had profited by his knowledge of the world, "What course should I pursue to obtain prosperity?" He replied, "Content-ment—if you are able, practise contentment."

Selman.

Translation - Everything's not perfect, but you can at least find *something* to be happy about. Focus on the good and appreciate what you have, not what you do not have.

True, we can always do more. It's hard not to experience this feeling, especially when dealing with children since they always seem to 'need' something—and indeed, at times, they really do. So a resulting anxiety can tug at you, often late into the night and your private life. Guard yourself against this inclination. Contentment is a state of happiness and satisfaction. On your way to doing more and finding prosperity, doing *less* may be the key. Strike a balance between ambition and contentment; peace and agitation; kindness and idleness. Contentment leads to prosperity, and prosperity leads to success and comfort. Do enough to feel contented about your service to your school and surrounding community, and make the rest of your time *yours*.

3.

THE foolish undertake a trifling act, and soon desist, discouraged; wise men engage in mighty works, and persevere.

Māgha.

Translation - You feel like quitting? Don't! That's what fools do. Giving up is for losers. Stay the course and see your mighty goal to the end, even if kids sleep, fight, and curse in class; even if they turned in a piece of homework with no name for the millionth time; even if they told their parents they turned in the project — but clearly didn't — and now mama bear is in your face. Press onward!

Fools take on meaningless and unimportant assignments. But we gather you are not a fool, at the very least because you are a teacher — a task that is highly important and meaningful. Pat yourself on the back! I think the lesson to take from here is this: minor aspirations do not generate the energy to persevere, not even for minor endeavors. To be wise means to apply learned knowledge or information. If you want to be a wise and valuable teacher, design a powerful mission statement this school year and see it through. Anything less will be a waste of your time. Be wise, my friend.

4.

THOSE who wish well towards their friends disdain to please them with words which are not true.

Bhāravi.

Translation - Keep it real and stop sugarcoating your feedback. If it sucks, tactfully tell them it sucks! Make sure you provide them a road map to better results.

While this quote regards friendship, I'd like to adapt it to a wider audience. We should promote the welfare of everyone; in the classroom context, that means our students, parents, and fellow teachers. We shouldn't lie to our friends and we shouldn't lie to those we work with and work for. Operating from truth and vulnerability can be scary, but they are essential elements to building trust. Progress can be rough—there are many pitfalls in that arena. However, lying to others simply to make them happy will almost certainly lead to ruin—both yours and theirs. If you really care about your students and constituents, love them and teach them, but do not spare them the necessary correction merely for temporary happiness.

5.

LIKE an earthen pot, a bad man is easily broken, and cannot readily be restored to his former situation; but a virtuous man, like a vase of gold, is broken with difficulty, and easily repaired.

Hitopadesa.

Translation - It's easier to forgive good people, so don't be a jerk.

There are two things you lose when you are a bad person: 1) Your reputation and 2) Your soul. Needless to say, your reputation goes a long way. Whether you are TOTY or a teacher on a professional development plan, your deeds tend to follow you. If you're one of the teachers who seldom—or never—hands in lesson plans, sponsors activities, or verbally abuses students, chances are you are not held in high regard at your school. Parents have immense difficulty reaching this person, their door is always closed, and staff members never ask them for help because they consider them useless. Been there...and sometimes, I've been that person. Burnout is very real! However, a poor reputation has consequences. It takes a long time to repair damage done and to right wrongs. When people speak against you, they will likely believe them over you. Why? Because you've failed to be virtuous—you're dishonorable. It's easy to break down something that already has cracks in it. But to do the right thing? Doing it consistently? Your name will be hard to tarnish and easy to mend. Stay the course! And if you've fallen off a little, get back on it!

6.

THE son who delights his father by his good actions; the wife who seeks only her husband's good; the friend who is the same in prosperity and adversity — these three things are the reward of virtue.

Bhartrihari.

Translation - When you display a high degree of character, students and faculty will seek to be in good standing with you. You'll receive all the invitations and calls when there's free food, fun programs in the auditorium, and after-school drinking sessions with your coolest coworkers.

There are three key takeaways: 1) Doing the right thing will foster a sense of pride in you and in others, 2) Want the best for others and 3) Be consistent and love through all. Take a moment right now to consider first how these virtues may be applied to your life, then how you can share these valuable and enriching concepts with others.

7.

LET us not overstrain our abilities, or we shall do nothing with grace. A clown, whatever he may do, will never pass for a gentleman.

La Fontaine.

Translation - Stay in your lane and do what you do best, and don't let the system make you break character. Don't sweat the small stuff!

Part of what makes magicians, athletes, and other high-performance individuals alluring is their ability to make the difficult appear effortless. But that effortlessness was produced by thousands of hours in the gym, studio, golf course, classroom, lab, etc. When you're trying too hard, that's a sign you are out of practice. While you can improve greatly, you cannot—and should not—make yourself in to something you are not. Every idea isn't an opportunity. Sometimes we overextend ourselves on a particular lesson, or balancing the many duties that come with our profession, and then burn out. You can only be who you are…and that's enough. The best version of you requires the least amount of effort.

NOTHING is more becoming a man than silence. It is not the preaching but the practice which ought to be considered as the more important. A profusion of words is sure to lead to error.

Talmud.

Translation - Say less. No, seriously... say less!

Spend less time talking and more time doing. Even with excellent command of a language, misinterpretations abound. What's harder to mishandle is the truth of what one is doing. Actions speak volumes. Between preaching and practicing, the latter is the more important and effective of the two. Get to work! The added benefit of not talking means you can do more listening.

9.

LET a man's talents or virtues be what they may, we feel satisfaction in his society only as he is satisfied in himself. We cannot enjoy the good qualities of a friend if he seems to be none the better for them.

Hazlitt.

Translation - Teach your students to love themselves. Generally, people love and respect you only as much you love and respect yourself.

Be happy with what you do. Choose friends who are happy with what they do. There's nothing worse than receiving a gift from someone who didn't want to give one, but it's always satisfying to delight in a gift and realize the giver is delighted in your delight. My point? Don't force someone to enjoy or engage in activities that don't bring them joy, no matter how talented they are. It's like seeing a tall person walking by and asking them if they play basketball. Regardless of the answer, their height is something for them to use, not you. Your satisfaction should come from the satisfaction they have in themselves. Here's a teacher application: praise a kid's effort, not the result.

A prudent man will not discover his poverty, his self-torments, the disorders of his house, his uneasiness, or his disgrace.

Hitopadesa.

Translation - Do what the job asks of you and nothing less. You can always do more, but doing less is asking for trouble.

Being prudent means thinking about your future, being wise and exercising common sense in regards to preparation, execution, and reflection. The teaching profession is a difficult one, but it grows even more difficult when we bring or allow trouble to our doorstep. We all know the teacher(s) complaining about student behavior, and we've all thought the same things, depending who it is: Is it *actually* the students, or is it poor classroom management? Planning the day's lesson while driving 80mph down the road, or not having a seating chart could be the culprit. Whatever bind you're in, exercise prudence and watch how you enter the classroom with more confidence, peace, and pride.

11.

MEN are of three different capacities: one understands intuitively; another understands so far as it is explained; and a third understands neither of himself nor by explanation. The first is excellent, the second, commendable, and the third, altogether useless.

Machiavelli.

Translation - Your usefulness is gauged by your level of understanding. Teachers must not only master their content areas, but also their emotional and somatic intelligence to be effective.

When you possess a certain level of knowledge, fewer things require thorough explanations. Always seek new information. Generate new ideas everyday!

When you're right on the cusp of a breakthrough, it helps to have someone who can get you across the line — think mentors, coaches, and friends. They can make things that you can't fully grasp crystal clear. In academia, it's important to nurture relationships with fellow colleagues and to build inroads to better understanding. There is nothing wrong with admitting you don't know some things. That opens the door for *others* to add value to *you*. So, start using your planning period! :)

When you don't *know* enough to see what you're missing or to *explain* what you need, you're in a dangerous position. A school led by such a person is likely in disarray and stinks of poor morale. Been there, done that, seen that, heard that. A lamentation situation or person like that can only highlight one thing: this person has not invested in themselves. While it's okay to rely on others sometimes, there's no hand more reliable than your own.

12.

WORLDLY fame and pleasure are destructive to the virtue of the mind; anxious thoughts and apprehensions are injurious to the health of the body.

Chinese.

Translation - All that glitters is not gold. Stop stressing over what you don't have, especially in the way of material possessions. Teaching won't make you rich- that's well-documented. There is no reason to die over that fact. Drink tea, work out, and cry in your car like everyone else. You're lucky because "You get summers off," they say.

Chill out, the world will still be here after you've had your meltdown. Frequent recognition and perpetual enjoyment can be corrosive to progress and happiness. Coveting certain lifestyles and material objects can promote anxiety and fearfulness. You may be a great teacher...but feel you're lacking because you haven't won TOTY; you may be a great coach...but you haven't brought your team a championship; you may be a tremendous principal...but the faculty turnover rate is still high. Let it go. Concentrate on the good. Believe you are more than what they see, and that you are more than the designer labels and plush car seats you envy—or that they are less fulfilling than you imagine them to be. Honor the power of the mind and realize you have a far greater mission than accumulating *stuff*. You've been entrusted with making *someone else's child* a more knowledgeable, global citizen full of character and drive.

13.

HUMAN experience, like the stern-lights of a ship at sea, illumines only the path which we have passed over.

Coleridge.

Translation - Hindsight is 20/20. So, there's no use crying over spilled milk; you live and you learn. The key is to fail better next time.

What we know and understand is extremely limited. Even if you've traveled far and wide, so much more of the world remains un-touched. It's important that when we deal with others, we under-stand that their level of perception is directly related to how much they've experienced through living, reading, or hearing—and vice versa. Forging a new frontier means going someplace you've never been. Meeting new people, reading more books, and trying new things will unearth regions you knew were there but couldn't quite articulate *where*. Judge less, love more. Travel more, talk less. The stern lights are behind you; meaning, understand your past…but look to the future with eyes not dimmed by the lights of before. Your students are children. Let them be children and make mis-takes. Every poor choice doesn't need to be met with a heavy hand.

MAN is an actor who plays various parts:

First comes a boy, then out a lover starts;

His garb is changed for, lo! a beggar's rags;

Then he's a merchant with full money-bags;

Anon, an aged sire, wrinkled and lean;

At last Death drops the curtain on the scene.

hartrihari.

Cf. Shakespeare:

"All the world's a stage," etc. —As You Like It, Act II, sc. 7.

Translation - We all deserve the opportunity to evolve. Life unfolds in stages, don't forget that. Where you are is not your final destination—neither is theirs.

This passage is both incredibly inspiring and comforting. Think about it- no matter where we start, we will not end in the same place...unless we want to. However, even that would be hard—finishing in the same exact spot. Aging is going to do most of the work, but that's something we can't help. However, *how* we get to—and through—each stage, will determine the look of our final scene and our closing remarks. Both you and your students are like caterpillars on your way to becoming butterflies. You are works-in-progress. There's a better teacher in you. There's another career down the road. There's a better student in that desk, and they'll have a beautiful family one day. Play your part until it's time to play another. Act it out the best you can. View yourself as a director when handling your students. Communicate your vision for the scene, then let them act it out. That's all you can do.

15.

MEN soon the faults of others learn,

A few their virtues, too, find out;

But is there one — I have a doubt —

Who can his own defects discern?

Sanskrit.

Translation - Stop being a hater and searching for others' weaknesses. That's lame. Take inventory of *your* life and improve *your* condition before picking apart another's.

It's easy to point out another's faults. Many of us have judgmental eyes and narrow minds; there are things in us that go unresolved and prompt us to solve ourselves by *solving others*. It says, "Men soon the faults of others learn." The word that stands out most to me here is *learn*. For whatever reason, we *study* others' faults, or study others long enough to *find* fault. Again, it's relatively easy to do. If someone is different than us — and most are — the differences become apparent pretty quickly. The way people chew, laugh, and talk may be minor annoyances, but picking apart someone and deciding what's good or bad in their behavior is something else entirely. If only we studied ourselves like we study our students, administration, or local government. Perhaps we'd discover that our observations are skewed in the direction of our tastes; meaning, your understanding of *fault* is based on your view of what's *right*. You may not always be in the right. Therefore, search out the best in others to help highlight areas to improve upon yourself.

16.

IN learning, age and youth go for nothing; the best informed take the precedence.

Chinese.

Translation - Just because you're older doesn't mean you're wiser!

If you work with children, you know at some point, they're going to do something wildly foolish. Your chin may hit the floor, blood may boil, or your sides will split with laughter, but it's inevitable…something ridiculous is always on the horizon. My point? When these things happen, we tend to dispense advice because we've *been around* longer. But learning doesn't necessarily come with age. Learning comes by knowledge and reflection, and that can happen at any age. Though they're going to struggle to understand some things that generally come with age, give them the best information available. They way you curb destructive behaviors or unwise antics is by making them the best informed individuals they can be. Guess what? In order to do that, *you* must also keep abreast of the latest trends, topics, and information pertaining to their academic and personal growth. Take some initiative and show some responsibility! Not all of us have been blessed with loving, dutiful, and encouraging parents. Those teachable moments are never worthless. They're worthwhile.

17.

AFFAIRS succeed by patience, and he that is hasty falleth headlong.

Sa'dī.

Translation - Haste makes waste, so don't wait until the last minute to prepare your lesson plans. Devote a few minutes a day to clearly-defined priorities and watch the stress evaporate when it's time to deliver.

One of the hardest concepts for people to understand is patience. It takes a while to find success. Losing weight, earning a degree, or training for a marathon all take considerable time, patience, and discipline before yielding tangible results. The same law applies in the classroom. Turning your school around is going to take time. Correcting classroom behavior won't happen overnight. Designing impactful lessons requires a little hit-and-miss. But that's how winners do it: they choose the long instead of the short. Get into the habit of making preparations, planning, executing, and refining your rituals. Imprint those principles onto your students' brains, and sit back over the next few months or years for your moment to beam with pride. If they hold the course, you might not recognize them. They'll be taller, somewhat more responsible and disciplined warriors capable of defeating any obstacle with time, effort, and coaching. But if *you* hold the course, you'll become someone worthy of being recognized…and that's a meaningful affair.

A man who has learnt little grows old like an ox: his flesh grows, but his knowledge does not grow.

Dhammapada.

Translation - You've changed but you haven't grown. Stop recycling lesson plans year after year and get with the times! Choose content over comfort.

Just because you're the adult, that doesn't make you right. I'm sure you know plenty of adults who *still* can't manage their finances, maintain healthy relationships, or choose healthier options in the grocery store. Age alone won't make you a sage. It's the learning that takes place along the way that grows knowledge. Schools should be about fostering a love for learning. Why? Everything requires it. Love takes learning. Careers demand learning. Happiness begs for learning. If you want the best future for you and your students, commit to learning *now* and not later. The lesson(s) you teach today may prevent a divorce down the line, or lead one of them towards a promotion or a new business. Take learning seriously, and think outside the box if you have to. Some things that we're *required* to teach are simply not fun. Break the rules a little. The best have learned to do that, and many times have had great success.

19.

NO one is more profoundly sad than he who laughs too much.

Richter.

Translation - You can laugh and smile but still have depression. Learn to deal with your problems in a healthy way. When that's done, learn to spot the warning signs in others. In short- watch over your students and colleagues. The school year is long, and sometimes we fall behind on grades, coach sports late into the evening, and fail to submit lesson plans on time. Don't suffer quietly with a smile. Ask for help and tip the scales back in your favor!

Mental health is critical. People, not just children, have an unhealthy relationship with social media and technology—not that these are solely responsible for personal illness—and possess unhealthy views about reality. Reality is your friend. Some things just *are*, and that's okay. But when that's not understood, we develop vices to cope with the harshness of the world. One of those ways can be laughing. Watch for students, friends, and family who are never sad, or seem to hide behind the laughter. It says no one is more *profoundly sad* than he who laughs too much. Don't be afraid to blow the whistle and alert a parent or counselor when you observe suspicious behavior. Better safe than sorry. Infuse a few lessons, if possible, on dealing with the stress of relationships, homework, or extracurricular activities.

20.

THIS world is a beautiful book, but of little use to him who cannot read it.

Goldoni.

Translation - Reading is a combination of recognizing and blending letters, remembering words and pronouncing them correctly, and comprehending their meaning when combined. We are not born knowing *how* to read, we must be *taught*. Yes, the world is beautiful, but if we do not seek instruction from those more skilled and apply that knowledge to gain further understanding of what life has to offer, we are lost. The beauty and the goodness of the world will pass right under your nose.

The world obeys a set of laws, if you will. While there are many languages across the globe, there's a universal language. I've traveled to more than 30 countries, and I can say for sure that there's a common thread across all cultures. If people like you where you are, generally, they will like you elsewhere. Smiles and manners translate worldwide. But if you don't, can't, or won't try to understand this, then the world will always be less enjoyable than fulfilling. There are keys or areas to opening up the world, such as constant learning, investing in relationships, serving others, and being authentic. If you can't do these things, there are doors that will remain closed to you forever, and that's not the life you want for your family or your students and coworkers. Model the secrets of the world to the undiscerning. Don't worry about the thanks, just keep serving. That means you've read the book!

21.

THE gem cannot be polished without friction, nor man perfected without trials.

Chinese.

Translation - Limit the number of retakes, makeups, extra credit, and other arbitrary assignments to bolster grades. Sometimes it's best to let them grow through adversity, which means letting them fail or designing rigorous projects. Hold their feet to the fire and you will draw out a sense of urgency, finality, and pride. Life doesn't always provide second chances, and there are fewer participation trophies in the real world. It's better they learn this early.

Part of teaching means polishing the rough spots and getting through the rough patches. Some students are buried deep within mountains of hurt, insecurity, or possibly privilege. Observing their trajectory and guiding their path involves taking a few branches to the face, or getting your brand new sneakers dirty. What does that look like? Breaking up fights, calling parents, talking with students after school, sponsoring a club when time is already scarce. It might mean spending a few extra hours differentiating lessons, or finding and creating meaningful content for the module. To perfect your students, you must challenge them, period. Otherwise, they'll never shine the way they were meant to…nor will you.

22.

CHOOSE knowledge, if thou desirest a blessing from the Universal Provider; for the ignorant man cannot raise himself above the earth, and it is by knowledge that thou must render thy soul praiseworthy.

Firdausī.

Translation - Everything you want is on the other side of *knowledge*. Coming by this knowledge may require pain, embarrassment, or prolonged waiting, but those experiences will strengthen your soul and empower you through the hard times as you attempt to elevate your position in the world.

Ever felt useless to a student? Maybe they approached you with a question, something pertinent for them…and you had no idea how to help them? Meanwhile, there are teachers others gravitate to and write beautiful speeches about. Those are individuals who have something valuable to impart. There's likely some knowledge that's being passed along that you do not have. In order for you to help yourself and others, you must choose knowledge and pursue it with great tenacity.

WHO aims at excellence will be above mediocrity; who aims at mediocrity will be far short of it.

Burmese.

Translation - Students will follow the arc you set for them, so define excellence and give them a rubric to guide them.

Mediocre is described as a state of poor quality, something or someone who is second-rate. It's imperative to remember that you are a professional and nothing about your practice should be amateurish or second-class; you have earned your degree and passed the content exam. Nevertheless, teachers often find themselves doing the bare minimum — we've all experienced those lulls — but hopefully that stems from exhaustion, not negligence. Again, it's easy to set your day — or maybe your week — on autopilot and coast to the weekend. Resist ease. You may have worksheets planned for each day, pair-work sessions and group projects scheduled, and a movie ready for Friday. Fight that temptation. Lazy teachers likely believe these students are getting the basic requirements established *by law*...but in reality it's probably far less. You risk becoming the 'fun' teacher, the teacher on a professional development plan, or the teacher whose classroom managements skills leave much to the imagination (upturned desks, incessant yelling, and Hot Cheeto bags on the floor).

Regardless, aiming for excellence will help mitigate those risks. Excellence protects you. On days you simply do not have the energy, your professional pedigree will speak for you. Students will excuse your fatigue and take over, administrators will understand leave days, and unsuccessful lessons will serve as learning opportunities because excellence is your goal; you recognize that your level of success is directly tied to your level of vision — which requires believing in the unseen, and your ability to manifest it.

However, what's unsaid is that you will *be* — meaning you will exist above mediocrity or far below it- when you *choose* to aim in either direction. Therefore, what you will become starts with what you see for yourself *and* your students.

24.

IF thy garments be clean and thy heart be foul, thou needest no key to the door of hell.

Sa'dī.

Translation - As the kids would say, "Keep it a buck!" This means tell the truth.

Demonstrate integrity in all you do. That means doing what you say you'll do, and saying what you mean. Kids recognize character better than anyone. *They* may not always display good character, but they certainly know what it is and what it looks like. Be genuine and consistent in the classroom. Admit when you've marked a test wrongly, or given students incorrect information. If you can't guarantee tests will be graded by a particular date, don't give them a definitive answer to begin with—even if they ask you a million times. Treat everyone fairly; they know when you're playing favorites—even if you can't see it. If you can't operate with integrity, there will be no need to invite chaos and bad omens into your life... your actions will have already done so.

25.

WE ought never to mock the wretched, for who can be sure of being always happy?

La Fontaine.

Translation - Don't kick people while they're down. Simple as that.

Don't delight in others' misery, even though it feels good sometimes. In most cases, it's just not worth it. They'll grow to resent you, and the joy you get from mocking them will be short-lived. You've lived long enough to know that you won't always be happy. It's an impossibility. What's not said here is that you should show compassion

36

because you understand happiness comes and goes, and *because* you can never be sure when the shoe will exchange feet. In the end, showing compassion *now* may gift you some later. Again, it says, "*Never* ...mock the wretched."

26.

A wise man adapts himself to circumstances, as water shapes itself to the vessel that contains it.

Chinese.

Translation - Go with the flow. If you've exceeded parameters on time but the students are engaged and having fun, go with it! If a student comes up with a great idea during a lesson, try it out! Your students have something to offer, too. So loosen up!

Much of your frustration comes from being inflexible. Sometimes we expect others to behave in the way *we think* they should, and when they don't? We become upset and angry, dangerous to others and ourselves. Try not to implement classroom policies that promote endless write-ups. No eating, drinking, talking, cheating, cursing, dancing, fighting, playing on the computer, playing on the phone, changing seats, standing up, not participating, etc. Veteran teachers understand which rules have more leeway than others. Wise teachers understand what to address and what not to, when to discipline and when not to. Remember: you run a classroom, not a prison.

On the other side of that, know every day will not be your day. You're going to have fire drills, professional development, random—or not so random- fights, observations, visitors in the building, etc. Be patient and observant. Watch for teachable moments and opportunities to serve the higher-ups valuable insights.

27.

HE who formerly was reckless and afterwards became sober brightens up this world like the moon when freed from clouds.

Dhammapada.

Translation - People can evolve, and even greater, utilize their newfound sagacity and capacity to loose others from the chains that imprisoned them. If you understand this, leading with compassion may be for you.

There are few things more gratifying than the evolved student. When you have the occasion to write positive notes home or make positive phone calls, it's a true joy. If you can be instrumental to your student's development, it's incumbent on your position to do so. Here are some ideas: 1). Appoint them a leadership role or let them collect/grade papers 2.) Talk with them 3). Recommend them for clubs or activities in the community. Brightening their world will radiate light on your doorstep as well.

28.

IF a man be not so happy as he desires, let this be his comfort — he is not so wretched as he deserves.

R. Chamberlain.

Translation - Have you met Murphy — as in Murphy's Law? It states: "Anything that can go wrong will go wrong." Keep that in mind when you're in a funk. Things could always be worse. So keep your fingers crossed!

Aren't we lucky we don't always get what we deserve? Lord knows I've done enough to land me in big trouble, but grace and mercy have protected me from myself, which I'm thankful for. Whatever you believe, grace and mercy are kindnesses that shed light on the dark places right in front of you. Where we are may be less than ideal, but if we knew what we'd been spared or had narrowly avoided, we might sing a new tune. It's cliche but things could always be worse. On the dreary days in the classroom or around the building, sing a song or bring a snack with you. I usually keep a drawer full of candy or chips to munch on when I'm out of it, and that usually brings me back to a good place. If you get the feeling a student is in the same place as you, share some with them too, but do it secretly, or else every student will swarm your desk when they hear your bag crinkle.

29.

IN conversation humour is more than wit, easiness, more than knowledge; few desire to learn, or to think they need it; all desire to be pleased, or, if not, to be easy.

Sir W. Temple.

Translation - Develop your social skills! Trust me when I say that people could not care less about your intelligence and ac-

complishments if you're a jerk. Seriously. People want to know if you can be a friend to them, and if you can make their lives easier with levity and unique perspective. That doesn't always mean *competence*; sometimes it just means *comfort*. So, be likable, my friend. Be likable.

Teaching ranks as one of the most stressful jobs in the United States. It's well-documented how dangerous stress can be; if you're not careful, it can even kill you. That being said, breaking up frustration and fatigue with humor is a good idea. Play games with students once in a while. Budget time at the end of class to unwind, or let students lead instruction in the way they want to. Take a step back and take it easy. Humor may not seem important but everyone enjoys resting, relaxing, and laughing. Use humor to break tension or introduce awkward topics of conversation. If you can teach them a lesson while telling a joke, you've found a winning situation. Take 2-3 minutes to share *the daily joke*; even better, assign students to tell a joke a day, or let their friend tell their joke. We all need a few laughs sometimes.

30.

TO reprehend well is the most necessary and the hardest part of friendship. Who is it that does not sometimes merit a check, and yet how few will endure one? Yet wherein can a friend more unfold his love than in preventing dangers before their birth, or in bringing a man to safety who is travelling on the road to ruin? I grant there is a manner of reprehending which turns a benefit into an injury, and then it both strengthens error and wounds the giver. When thou chidest thy wandering friend do it secretly, in season, in love, not in the ear of a popular convention, for oftentimes the presence of a multitude makes a man take up an unjust defence, rather than fall into a just shame.

Feltham.

Translation - Stop letting things slide when they should not! I know, hallways and classrooms are filled with inappropriate behavior and language, and it's difficult to monitor, much less discipline all the offenders. Phones are out when they're not supposed to be, wrappers crinkle during lessons, and heads are down during instruction. Oh, I get it! You still need to adminis-

ter justice though times are bleak. Do it because you love them. Do it because it will prevent future danger. Do it because a *just* shame is an excellent teacher.

One of the most challenging tasks as a teacher is administering discipline. If you love the students or your school, you have to speak up and check those who are out of line—no matter who they are. However, tact is key. Don't embarrass students in front of the class or act petty, but shoot an occasional zinger. We've all been there. Kids can run you up a wall and, at a certain point, you're liable to do or say anything—or at least you feel that way. Since you care about them, you correct them in private, with love. It's difficult to dispense wisdom when you're angry or frustrated. Discipline is a challenging art form, and the hardest part of both teaching and friendship. You may have to take a few moments to prepare yourself and gather your remarks. Just tell yourself that what you're doing is for the best.

31.

HE who seeks wealth sacrifices his own pleasure, and, like him who carries burdens for others, bears the load of anxiety.

Hitopadesa.

Translation - Wealth doesn't equate to pleasure; it's simply a vehicle you obtain to drive you where you really want to go. However, it's the pressure you place on yourself to win, succeed, and monopolize that generates undue stress, and is ultimately your undoing. Maybe we should teach our students how to be happy...instead of teaching them to land a job to be happy.

Sometimes we stress over the wrong things, like who gets the credit or who has the best scores in the department. You sacrifice a lot of peace that exists in the present in favor of worrying about things out of your control—like future events.

32.

CIRCUMSPECTION in calamity; mercy in greatness; good speeches in assemblies; fortitude in adversity: these are the self-attained perfections of great souls.

Hitopadesa.

Translation - Whether you like it or not, you're a role model and are expected never to go beyond the pale. It's hard to do that *all the time,* and can lead to pretty rowdy weekends when you're off-duty. But let's face it, the students are using you as a barometer of decency, character, and professionalism. Don't waste your opportunity to dazzle them with a great speech once in a while to show strength and peace in chaos, and to respond to ugliness with kindness and mercy—to forgive. You're the teacher. Never forget that.

While there's no perfect definition of what a 'great soul' is, these attitudes and actions are a 'great' start. When things go wrong, it is important to analyze where you went wrong, to think on your mindset and the way the situation played out. Doing so may lead to shining the spotlight on ourselves and administering a little self-compassion. On the other side, we may require a bit of mercy—controlled by those in power or with the advantage—to survive our follies. Granting mercy after victory demonstrates a love that is undeserved...which makes the gesture all the more meaningful. Still, mercy isn't only for the weak; even the strong require mercy. Power and advantage carry much weight, and those who wield them don't always distribute them equally or fairly though it's perceived as fair to them. In those moments, staying strong despite disappointment and adversity will become extremely important to your personal development. Make a good speech to the perpetrator(s) and move on. Later, work on the attributes that will empower you and ingratiate you to others in the future.

33.

THE best preacher is the heart; the best teacher is time; the best book is the world; the best friend is God.

Talmud.

Translation - Between God and the world stands *your heart* and *your time*. Preach, teach, read, and love. This is how you live life the best.

Preachers sermonize the Gospel with oratory prowess and conviction. Similarly, you must deliver your lessons with conviction from the heart. They won't know the lesson means something unless it means something to you.

Time has been with all of us since we were born. Undoubtedly, we've all been corrected by hindsight. What you cannot instill today, leave for time. Give students a chance to evolve. You are not the key to every door. If a student, parent, or administrator is troublesome, leave that relationship or that person's development to someone else. Leave it to time. Time has a way of restoring balance.

Books merely encompass what's in the world, or what's in the mind of someone who is in the world. Living, playing, and working in the world allows you to *read* others and to *read* your own story. Open yourself to the possibilities that lie in the unexplored. It's likely there are colleagues with whom you've never spoken to, or students you seldom call on. Ask more questions, take more field trips, and commit to more personal and professional development. Improving yourself will increase your value to others.

Whether or not you're religious, there's this little voice in your head that is always with you, always talking, always listening. Consider this person your best friend. Monitor your self-talk. When times are difficult, consult and counsel yourself with kindness and mercy. We are often our own worst enemies when it comes to exchanges with others or achieving our goals. Keep your mind and your heart fixed on your values, on principles in your religious text, or on the virtues you appreciate in others.

34.

A woman will not throw away a garland, though soiled, which her lover gave: not in the object lies a present's worth, but in the love which it was meant to mark.

Bhāravi.

Translation - Do all things with *spirit*. Let whatever is guiding you underneath make its way to the surface. We want to see the real you, and what's really motivating your interactions with us. We hope to discover you really do care for us.

I'm reminded of a quote by Maya Angelou: "I've learned that people will forget what you said, people will forget what you did, but people will never forget how you made them feel." Reaching students and parents isn't easy, but it becomes easier when the message you're delivering comes from a true place...from the heart. When your intentions are good, even your losses can work in your favor. Therefore, despite rowdy parents and apathetic students, put on your best face and remember what your purpose is; it's not to make everyone happy—you are not there for their happiness, but for their success. Act with love and good intent. Design your lessons with meaning and drive them home with charisma. They may miss the message, but they'll pick up on your passion...and that passion may be the seed to explosive growth in the future. That holds true for discipline, instruction, and advice.

THERE are three whose life is no life: he who lives at another's table; he whose wife domineers over him; and he who suffers bodily affliction.

Talmud.

Translation - Unless you take control of your situation, your life will belong to someone else. So, don't let the students, staff, or parents walk all over you.

Take control of your life- that's the theme expressed here in these three scenarios. You must be able to stand on your own and not always rely on others. Nothing but resentment grows from such inequity. Do you know someone who always asks for money, always needs a ride somewhere, or always complains and uses you as a soundboard? Yeah, it's not very fun. That leads into the second point- don't be a pushover. Stand up for yourself. Parents are going to fight hard—damn hard—to elevate their child's grade, or cover for their irresponsibility and poor choices. The system encourages them to disregard the rules and make waves until the teacher or principal concedes, not wanting a scandal or reprisal. Nevertheless, hold your ground. Align yourself with truth and leave it at that. This way, your hands will always be clean, even if things don't work out the way they should. Lastly, take care of yourself. Much of life is having the health to enjoy it. Take a mental health day every once in a while to stay home and do nothing. Play music during your planning period, or during the work period while students are in groups, taking a test, or working silently. Walk around the building for a few minutes, or step outside during lunch and feel the sun on your face. If you're having a rough week, share how you feel with students and colleagues. They may ask how they can help, or be more forgiving when you accidentally flip your lid.

In review: 1) Stand on your own two feet 2) Stand up for yourself 3). Take a stand for your mental health and personal happiness.

36.

LET thy words between two foes be such that if they were to become friends thou shouldst not be ashamed.

Sa'dī.

Translation - Don't burn your bridges. Words create scars that take a lot longer to heal than physical wounds. So, it's better to say less when encountering stressful situations in and out of the building.

This one is deep! Have you ever been so angry or frustrated that you just said whatever came to your mind at the time, no matter how ugly? Yeah, we've all been there, and in the teaching profession we can find ourselves there a lot. I've been guilty of this, and that's why I can tell you the following embarrassment is difficult to live down—you feel naked, ashamed of your mouth and lack of self-control. Oftentimes, after blow-ups like those, a kind of friendship or connection develops, whether small or large. Every time you get together, you're reminded of each other's past behavior. To bring it into full view: we've snapped at children and felt naked as a jay bird after doing so. The student is hot in the face, droopy-eyed, head on the desk with their lips poked out. Moments ago, you felt justified in your verbal assault, but now you're just frustrated and disappointed in yourself. In the future, take a breather, gather yourself, and then say what you need to say in the way you need to say it. You're a teacher, a professional, and a role model. But more than that? You're a human being and you're going to make mistakes. The most responsible thing you can do is make a note of this, and redirect your efforts to acting in this way when future challenges arrive. Essentially, you've created an intervention strategy for yourself, haha.

37.

THERE never was, there never will be, a man who is always praised, or a man who is always blamed.

Dhammapada.

Translation - Take everything in stride. Even your best students can act out of character; conversely, your most problematic students can surprise you. Drink wine and meditate on this. Or just drink lots of wine.

Everyday won't be your day. Serena Williams does not win every match. Mike Trout does not win every game. Stephen Curry does not hit every shot. Conversely, there are days when they are on fire and seem unstoppable. What we can learn from sports — or pretty much any other area in life — is that you have to take the good with the bad. One day you're a student's favorite teacher. The next? A sworn enemy. This year, you're Teacher of the Year. Next year? You weren't even nominated. Everyone patted you on the back for winning the state football championship last year. This year, the team's not doing well and everybody's blaming you- the coach. People are fickle. It is what it is. So, don't get too high or too low when your moment comes. Keep pushing forward, and know the pendulum will soon swing the other way.

A good man's intellect is piercing, yet inflicts no wound; his actions are deliberate, yet bold; his heart is warm, but never burns; his speech is eloquent, yet ever true.

Māgha.

Translation - There's more than one way to skin a cat. Accomplish what's necessary without inflicting harm. In other words, be decisive and authoritative but tactful.

There's a way to conduct yourself in both adversity and your winning season. Winners are bold strategists and savvy executioners. They walk with great balance between the light and the dark, knowing when to be assertive and when to fall back. There's a way to be the smartest person in the room without being pompous. You can effect change when your heart and mind are clear. You can speak to the root of a matter without being callous and rude. The quote begins with, "A good man's," meaning this is what good people do. Staff and students are always watching. Don't give them a reason to question your character or professionalism, but give them every reason to trust and rely on your strength, intelligence, and integrity.

39.

TREES loaded with fruit are bent down; the clouds when charged with fresh rain hang down near the earth: even so good men are not uplifted through prosperity. Such is the natural character of the liberal.

Bhartrihari.

Translation - As Shakespeare communicated in Henry IV, Pt 2., "Uneasy lies the head that wears a crown." As their favorite teacher, an influential leader in the department, or the biggest-winning coach in the building, you just have to accept that significant hurdles and pain points come with the territory.

'LOADED with fruit,' and ' CHARGED with fresh rain,' signal grand purpose and ability. The greater the gift, the greater the burden. Your expertise is incomparable and your mission is ordained by the heavens... except fulfilling your destiny is hard. You feel like you struggle more than others or people are always coming to you, and because of that, you seldom have time alone. Colleagues fail to do their part because they know you can and will carry them for the sake of the team. The head of your department counts on you year-after-year to deliver top-notch test scores. Don't lament the burden. Instead, appreciate the faith they've placed in you. They wouldn't call on you if you didn't possess something they did not have themselves. Your intelligence, patience and charisma shine best when times are dark; that's when you're needed most—in times of crisis. Consequently, this is when you receive the most praise. So, sponsor that club, stay late, help someone with their lesson plan, or chaperone a school outing. How else will they know of your greatness unless you show them?

40.

THE man who neither gives in charity nor enjoys his wealth, which every day increases, breathes, indeed, like the bellows of a smith, but cannot be said to live.

Hitopadesa.

Translation - Live your life! Decide who you're going to be as a teacher and embrace it to the fullest. Give freely and celebrate yourself often. Teachers may not be well-paid, but that doesn't mean there's nothing to gain. Know that you're rich; know that giving and gratitude make you truly wealthy.

Read carefully. It says the man who NEITHER gives NOR enjoys his wealth cannot be said to live. What a distinction! You're alive when you're giving, you're alive when you're enjoying your wealth, but you cease living when you are doing neither. Notice it does not mention money. Giving in charity can mean donating time, advice, or resources. Enjoying your wealth could mean celebrating health or nurturing relationships. Teachers are unique in that we can give all the time. We have hundreds of students who need our charity, and require our wealth of information and perspective. But when we fail to do both, we don't live...and neither do they.

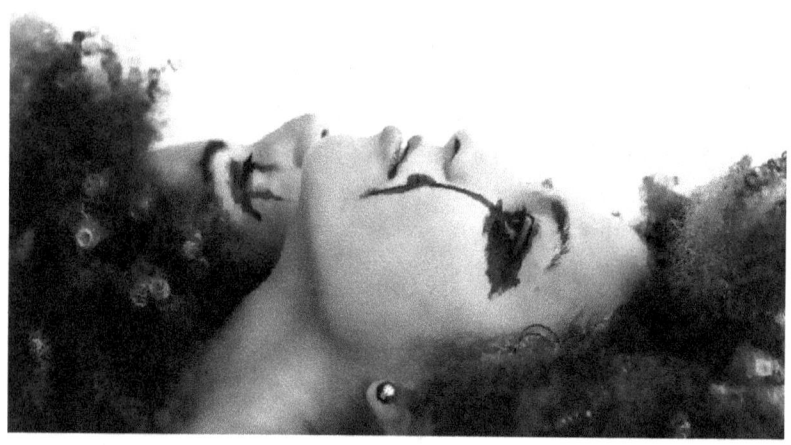

41.

THERE is not half so much danger in the desperate sword of a known foe as in the smooth insinuations of a pretended friend.

R. Chamberlain.

Translation - Everyone's not your friend. I repeat, there are squares in your inner circle. That nosy teacher who's always telling other people's business? Yeah, she's telling yours, too. Keep your eyes open, your ears to the ground, and don't give them anything to talk about.

Everyone's not your friend. Remember Michael Corleone in Godfather 2–"Keep your friends close, but your enemies closer." Why would he say this? Because your friends have known you for years. You call, text, and FaceTime regularly. They've shared meals at your home and vice versa. With so much access and knowledge, close proximity is the perfect place to conceal nefarious motives—

and enemies know that! This is why kids butter you up when their grade is low, and why parents drop off gifts throughout the school year. You can at least respect the students who relay their disdain for you face-to-face. No guessing there. However, sly coworkers and shifty students have mastered the art of small talk and volunteering. Don't let them trick you with their coded lines and smooth behavior. Friends will love you no matter what, but your enemies will not.

42.

ALL kinds of beauty do not inspire love: there is a kind of it which pleases only the sight, but does not captivate the affections.

Cervantes.

Translation - You are truly a difference maker, and the way you make your largest impact and leave an enduring legacy is to share with them something they can get nowhere else: the real you. You are a brand no one else can copy, so wear yourself proudly.

All kinds of beauty do not inspire love, and all kinds of teaching do not inspire change or progress. There's a certain level of teaching that meets the minimum requirements—where lesson plans are uploaded, classroom is set up, grades are turned in on time, and calls home are being made. However, there's another level of teaching, one that goes beyond 'the book.' I believe that secret ingredient is intent- positive intent rooted in the heart. It's the same for beauty. Sometimes there's a minor detail that makes all the difference—the difference between hand-made and coming off the factory line. If you wish to win the affections of your students, parents, and colleagues, the details will be your key to opening that door. Instead of passing out candy on holidays and after tests, try giving away books or tickets to free events. That's different. That will get you noticed. That's a gift that has valuable beyond the immediate.

CONTENTMENT consisteth not in heaping more fuel, but in taking away some fire.

Fuller.

Translation - It's okay to let the kids have a free day once in a while, to let the fire breathe a little. In a world where bell-to-bell instruction is the motto, it's okay to ignore the system sometimes and set aside the last 10 minutes for play. You'll be happier and so will they.

Less is more. In nearly every area of life, having less or doing less is prized. We're encouraged to eat less in one sitting, or enjoy smaller meals throughout the day. We're advised to stop dating around and find a husband or wife. Spend less and save more, consolidate your closet, limit the number of options when making choices. There's the law of diminishing returns, where the benefits gained are less than what you put in. At a certain point, that new fragrance is exciting and you spray it on for nearly every event. But after a while, the newness wears off and you find yourself perusing the perfume aisle.

Hint - Give your lesson plans a boost by doing less, not requiring less. Place the lesson in the students' hands and watch them work. Alleviate your workload by asking for assistance from colleagues, students, and parents. Choose one day a week to call parents, not everyday. Set strict office hours. Close your door. Assign a classroom leader who acts in your stead. Simplify classroom procedures. Instead of ten classroom rules, make it three—and make them important!

I think you get my drift.

IT is difficult to personate and act a part long, for where truth is not at the bottom Nature will always be endeavouring to return, and will peep out and betray herself one time or other.

Tillotson.

Translation - Ever spot a counterfeit item? Whether it's a designer handbag, a pair of Jordans, or a luxury perfume, there's always something that indicates it's a fake; when you know what to look for, it becomes even more apparent. It's the same in teaching. Your department head and administrators can tell when you're faking the funk, and vice versa. For better or worse, be unapologetically you. Better the devil we know.

Be yourself. Why? Because being disingenuous is exhausting! We sometimes paint ourselves into corners by putting on certain faces. You're the teacher everyone confides in, but in reality, you're disinterested and just want to go home to pour a glass of wine. Maybe you're a teacher who hates teaching... but it's how you pay the rent, so you put on a happy face (maybe), attend meetings on time, and input grades regularly—all the while you're stressed inside, curse all the way to work, and sprint to your car at 3:30. Notice what it says, "It is difficult to personage and act a part *long*." We all can pretend for a while, but it's hard to act the part of what's not in us. *Nature* will always return—that includes us. The seasons return every year. The sun rises and sets in the same cardinal directions every day. And the person you really are inside is aching to betray your daily facade. Do everyone a favor and be yourself, even if it means leaving the teaching profession. Both parties are likely to be made happier by this choice.

IT is better to be well deserving without praise than to live by the air of undeserved commendation.

R. Chamberlain.

Translation - The undeserving seem to get everything! Annnnd-dddd it's true. But you know what? Be great anyway and live in the shadows like the superhero you are.

Chamberlain said a lot here! There are so many ways this could be interpreted. All of your efforts won't be applauded or recognized-so just accept it. Do not hinge your value on recognition, nor seek praise. Stand resolute in that your efforts garner their own merits, visible or not. Move forward. Do not envy those who do less but receive more. If you're a teacher reading this, you are fully aware the best often go unnoticed. The bookkeeper is the unsung hero at your school. The assistant coach stayed longer and studied harder than the head coach. The assistant principal was doing both her job *and* the principal's. Such is life. Trust that it will be enough. Live by *your* standards, not theirs.

46.

NEVER put thyself in the way of temptation: even David could not resist it.

Talmud.

Translation - Temptation is a boulder cascading downhill. Don't invite storms that have rains you cannot weather. Leave your classroom door open when talking with students, don't drive anyone home, and don't be too friendly. It doesn't take much for something to be interpreted incorrectly. Even the wise sometimes act on false flags. You've been warned.

Never. Talmud begins this valuable idea with *never*. The next critical piece is *put thyself*- meaning *we* place *ourselves* in danger. I agree with that. When it says to never put yourself in the way of temptation, that conjures up an image of temptation moving like a locomotive, and we should steer clear from the rails to let the smoking contraption pass. Talmud even references King David. David sent Bathsheba's husband to the frontlines—presumably, to die—so that he could steal his wife. Every option is not an opportunity. It would be wise to recognize the difference.

47.

BY six qualities may a fool be known: anger, without cause; speech, without profit; change, without motive; inquiry, without an object; trust in a stranger; and incapacity to discriminate between friend and foe.

Arabic.

Translation - When I first read this quote, I thought of nearly every teenager I've taught. Haha, seriously. But if we're honest, this sounds like many adults, too. Temper your hubris and polish your uncultivated qualities.

A fool is an unwise person. There are some not-so-nice substitutes for the word fool, but that's because I believe foolishness is a set of thoughts and choices that often leads to damning or embarrassing consequences. In order to avoid such a fate, let's analyze the six qualities that lead to foolishness by asking questions-

Anger without cause. What makes you angry? How often are you angry? Is anger warranted in this case? Is there a more helpful emotion or perspective available here?

Speech without value. Are the students gaining something from your speech(es), book(s), or video(s)? Is this a moment where saying less could actually have more of an impact? Do I know enough to join this conversation?

Change without motive. What inspired the change? Was this change necessary? What was gained or lost from it? Do you anticipate a following change? Was this change for you? Can you go back?

Inquiry without an object. Am I thinking for the sake of thinking, or am I really trying to solve something? Am I just being nosy, or do I have a valid reason for my inquest? What do you think about when there's nothing to think about?

Trust in a stranger. Hopefully, we all understand this doesn't mean distrust strangers—because I've met many strangers who've helped me in the grocery store, at work, and in the gym when I nearly dropped the bench press bar on my chest. What it does mean, however, is to not place your faith in someone who has not been verified by you or someone you trust. It would be foolish to gamble your career on something you heard a student or colleague said without knowing much about their character. It's okay to believe in others, just verify your hunches to be safe.

Incapacity to discriminate between friend and foe. This one has as much to do with knowing others as it does knowing yourself. Our ability to interpret others is influenced by how well we know ourselves and who we hang around. Friends and foes can do nice things for you and *appear* to support you, but the difference is how you feel at the end of those engagements. Are you happier? Are you worried? Are you questioning the way something happened, or does something not match up? Chances are, you're right. So hone your instincts and vet your friends and acquaintances—not out of distrust, but of prudence. Reflect on some of the things that may be blocking you from seeing clearly, such as money, love, or anger. The best advice I can give you is this- not only have your friends have been with you through your victories, but also your losses.

48.

MEN are not to be judged by their looks, habits, and appearances, but by the character of their lives and conversations. 'Tis better that a man's own works than another man's words should praise him.

Sir R. L'Estrange.

Translation - Challenge your students to turn out quality work that speaks for itself. They should know beforehand what level of work they've submitted, making the grading process a mere formality. Similarly, a teacher's pedigree should shine through in their instruction, and less via word-of-mouth. If you do it right, the degree of quality in your work should slightly outshine the praise lauding your masterpiece. One direction is better than the other.

Both pubic and private education sometimes seem to thrive off ornamentation; meaning, the prevailing narratives and initiatives value looks over substance. Each year, there are new programs, new summer reading lists, new t-shirts, new mantras...and yet, the same old problems often persist. Why? Character relates to one's mental and moral qualities. This is how we're judged, not by that other stuff. Ask yourself - Does my school have character? Do my coworkers choose the moral high ground? What is the quality of my students' thinking skills? What are the trending conversations in the hallways, offices, and classrooms? What if an alien landed on campus and decided to take a tour- what would they hear and see? This is how you are judged, so mind your conversations and your principles. Kids aren't always excellent doers...but they are incredible watchers!

49.

TO exert his power in doing good is man's most glorious task.

Sophocles.

Translation - Devoting your energy to spreading positivity in the world ensures your name will live on beyond that time and place. Good deeds are like dandelion spores blown into the breeze, destined to beautify a distant patch of earth and curing the land of barrenness.

Never stop doing good just because it doesn't appear to yield tangible or real-time results. These days, doing the right thing or being helpful can seem like a chore. Trust me, I get it. I've sponsored three after-school clubs at once! But the keyword here is 'exert', meaning to make a physical or mental effort. To rehash the quote- doing good can be exhausting. I believe Sophocles chose his words carefully, and that exert is exactly the right word for the occasion. Make the extra effort this year! Perform at your highest level when you're stressed, uncertain, physically fatigued, or in a rut of some kind. That's how you become worthy of admiration. That's where the glory is.

TIME is the most important thing in human life, for what is pleasure after the departure of time? and the most consolatory, since pain, when pain has passed, is nothing. Time is the wheel-track in which we roll on towards eternity, conducting us to the Incomprehensible. In its progress there is a ripening power, and it ripens us the more, and the more powerfully, when we duly estimate it. Listen to its voice, do not waste it, but regard it as the highest finite good, in which all finite things are resolved.

Von Humboldt.

Translation - Whatever the task, whatever the passion- stick with it long enough to reveal the promise of the endeavor. While we cannot control time, we *can* master how we use it to create or sharpen existing skills. Therefore, it's on you to manipulate time in the classroom and wield it for your and your students' good. Design lessons that aid them both now and later into the twilight of their years.

Reread the first line: TIME is the most important thing in human life. No matter which path we take, time is the dirt beneath our feet; and every step we take—in any direction—will cover more dirt, or more time. We are walking towards eternity, but must live in the here and now. On that road to the Incomprehensible, I believe we must do good along the way. You are a teacher. You have been assigned the monumental task of shaping a human life. You are the sun, rain, and nutrients that will help to sharpen and ripen your students. Don't waste such an opportunity. Utilize your time to listen to the highest good within yourself and in others, and then enact that wisdom with the remaining time. Remember: You are important. Time will reveal that.

51.

ALL that we are is made up of our thoughts; it is founded on our thoughts, it is made up of our thoughts. If a man speak or act with a pure thought, happiness will follow him, like a shadow that never leaves him.

Dhammapada.

Translation - Our lives are shaped by the quality of our thinking. It is up to us to design and manage our thoughts so that we can better carve a path towards happiness and fulfillment. Nature is neither inherently good nor inherently bad, but through our perspective and behavior, we make it one way or the other. Therefore, choose virtue and know that what you put into motion will eventually find its way back to you.

Take control of your thoughts. This is one area you control completely. As teachers, we tend to act as receivers taking on info from various channels, and it can get overwhelming. It's easy to lose yourself—that inner voice guiding your day-to-day activities and routines. Work hard to focus on your inner conversations. If you're not careful, you can make yourself sick. Alternatively, you can also make yourself healthier and happier. Change your 'inner conversation,' and notice how your outer ones will follow.

52.

ANGER that has no limit causes terror, and unseasonable kindness does away with respect. Be not so severe as to cause disgust, nor so lenient as to make people presume.

Sa'dī.

Translation - Find a happy medium in the classroom. Respect is a difficult road to navigate. The best way to earn it is through consistency. Update grades regularly, don't make excuses, discipline students according to school policy and classroom rules, and check your attitude at the door. This way students won't expect privileges they haven't earned.

It would be easy to say yelling isn't always the way...but sometimes it is. The keyword here though is 'limit'. Keep your anger in a healthy state, one warranted and rooted in constructive criticism. The minute anger arrives, squash it by asking yourself this question: "Why am I so upset right now?" Hint - The answer should cast light on both you and the subject. However, replacing anger with unmitigated kindness won't do, either. Don't let students run over you because you're afraid of confrontation or a pesky parent. You don't want them discovering you're a wolf without fangs. Your best bet is simply to set the tone early and lead with heartfelt correction. Authenticity and consistency are key here. They will not only unlock success, but also much more.

Bonus.

That's all 52! Thank you for making it this far, and I hope you en-joyed the first release in the F.O.R. series (Facing Obstacles Realis-tically) - Teacher Edition. The follow-up to this is *For Students*, translating another 52 quotes into student-speak while providing a little wisdom.

As a bonus, I've added a few more quotes to get you through to graduation. Some of you may have exhausted this by Christmas break! Yikes, hang in there! We've all had tough semesters, multi-ple preps, or time-intensive responsibilities outside of the classroom, like clubs, sports, and leadership assignments. Tackle one day at a time and listen to your body. I'm serious.

Take your time with the rest of these and refer to this when your double shot of espresso isn't quite enough, okay?

Best,

Nicholas

MOST men, even the most accomplished, are of limited faculties; every one sets a value on certain qualities in himself and others: these alone he is willing to favour, these alone will he have cultivated.

Goethe.

Translation - You work on the skills you believe are valuable. No one is exceptional at everything; instead we shine in the areas we devote our efforts to. But what that also means is that there are unexplored territories within us that could also serve us greatly. Don't focus too much on your strengths without considering the usefulness of a cultivated weakness.

Make a plan today to sharpen your strengths. You don't have to be good at everything, but make certain you further sharpen your skills—iron against iron. Don't take the easy road this week. Encourage your peers to challenge themselves this week with airtight, student-centered lesson plans. Stick to your strengths and mine the students for theirs. Help them realize their value by forcing them to ask what makes them click. Who they are is, in part, influenced by what they focus on. Knowing that, reassigning core principles and magnifying others will become extremely important over the course of the semester.

54.

THE best thing is to be respected, the next, is to be loved; it is bad to be hated, but still worse to be despised.

Chinese.

Translation - There's an order to surviving in the education system. More and more, teachers are being asked to take on responsibilities that belong to the parents—providing school supplies, teaching social skills, keeping up with medical records, etc. The distance between love and hate, and respect and contempt is measured by how one handles the duties assigned to them. Execute your orders, and demand others follow through with theirs as well.

Gaining your students' or coworkers' respect can be challenging. Sometimes it won't matter what you do, as your actions simply won't translate to more admiration or more trust. When that happens, don't envy other classrooms and schools. Know that hate and love aren't far from each other, and that it's better to be disliked and hated than to be avoided all together.

55.

IF you injure a harmless person, the evil will fall back upon you, like light dust thrown up against the wind.

Buddhist.

Translation - Antagonizing a student or colleague simply isn't worth it. Stooping to their level will land you in hot water, and possibly ruin the reputation you've worked so hard to craft. Actually, there's a psychological term known as displacement, where we transfer our feelings to another. Be mindful of this when dealing with innocent students and faculty members. They're not the ones who hurt you.

We've all said things we didn't mean, but it can be particularly painful when a barb is misdirected and strikes an innocent bystander. Unfortunately, our private lives can bleed into our professional lives. When that happens, understand the injuries you inflict will revisit you one day to open fresh wounds. Be quick to apologize, and be genuine.

56.

IN the life of every man there are sudden transitions of feeling, which seem almost miraculous. At once, as if some magician had touched the heavens and the earth, the dark clouds melt into the air, the wind falls, and serenity succeeds the storm. The causes which produce these changes may have been long at work within us, but the changes themselves are instantaneous, and apparently without sufficient cause.

Longfellow.

Translation - Redemption is waiting around the corner! Whether a change in fortune needs your assistance or not, you can count on ordinary miracles to deliver you into your winning season when you least expect it. See, there's hope for the student you can't stand :)

Believe change is afoot! One of the hardest things we witness, as educators, is students repeatedly making the same mistakes. We get the same old attitudes, lack of effort, and disinterest... and it makes it hard to treat everyone fairly and with kindness. Sometimes, we even play favorites just to help us make it through the day, or get a lesson to run smoothly. I get it, I do. Still, how would you treat them if you knew their breakthrough was right around the corner?

MAN is an intellectual animal, therefore an everlasting contradiction to him-self. His senses centre in himself, his ideas reach to the ends of the universe; so that he is torn in pieces between the two without the possibility of its ever being otherwise. A mere physical being or a pure spirit can alone be satisfied with itself.

Hazlitt.

Translation - Make peace with your students and their parents, colleagues, administrators, and the education system. Everything we enjoy is run by people, and people are flawed. People are walking contradictions. If you allow for chaos, peace will find you much faster. Trust your spirit but keep your feet rooted in the ground.

The education system is going to change every couple years. A new program will be unfurled, or a new initiative will breakout and cause widespread angst and a few cheers... but mostly angst. Haha. Children, staff, and parents are going to be wishy-washy and drive you up the wall with their inconsistency. To counter this, strengthen your body and your spirit. Eat right, exercise, read, and reflect. Harmony is elusive…but not meaningless.

58.

IF thou desirest that the pure in heart should praise thee, lay aside anger; be not a man of many words; and parade not thy virtues in the face of others.

Firdausī.

Translation - It's not *what* you do but *how* you do it. The right type of praise and attention is what's key here. Your colleagues see you, believe me. Whatever virtues you exude, they're well-known. Humility and compassion cloak and protect leaders much better than vanity and indignation. Remember, birds of a feather…

Less is more. All things do not have to be said. And if they must? Deliver your words with empathy and grace. Show your coworkers, students, and community who you are through your strength of character. Let your actions speak. That way, when you do have something to say, they will be ready and anxious to listen.

59.

THE fish dwell in the depths of the waters, and the eagles in the sides of heaven; the one, though high, may be reached with the arrow, and the other, though deep, with the hook; but the heart of man at a foot's distance cannot be known.

Burmese.

Cf. Proverbs, XXV, 3.

Translation - Don't judge a book by its cover. The quietest student has so much to say. The rowdiest student is waiting to be tamed. The struggling student is one lesson away from dazzling you. Be creative and patient when it comes to reaching others.

Your students are deeper than you can fathom. They have genius that has not yet been realized. So do you! Look beyond the immaturity and the fights; beyond the laughter and the tears; and beyond the poor or stellar marks. Who they are today- they will not be that person forever. So, love them and treat them as if they're your guardian angels. They just may be. Ask yourself right now: What can I do to draw out their superpowers?

60.

THE life of man is the incessant walk of nature, wherein every moment is a step towards death. Even our growing to perfection is a progress to decay. Every thought we have is a sand running out of the glass of life.

Feltham.

Translation - Everything has a life cycle—animals, plants, people, products…even your career. Everything we do is flowing somewhere, so why not direct our efforts with the timelessness of the infinite? Build yourself and your students up to stand the test of the time. While you will pass on at some point, ideas never die.

Everything is playing out as it should. Every situation doesn't require your interference. Everyone doesn't need your advice. Let the chips fall where they may, and be okay with that. Use your time wisely. Concentrate your energy on being the best you can be, and when it's all said and done, you will have built something that will be harder to erode in the years to come.

61.

I have observed that as long as a man lives and exerts himself he can always find food and raiment, though, it may be, not of the choicest description.

Goethe.

Translation - Push yourself! The energy and motivation you need is all around you- you just have to search for it. Let the kids grade their own assignments, appoint a classroom leader, employ the assistance of a teacher across the hall or next door. Be creative and steadfast to secure that extra pack of copy paper!

Some days are gonna suck, and there's no way around it. Still, you need to push through! Your efforts may not manifest into your deserved harvest, but something is better than nothing, as hard as that is to hear. Live to fight another day. Put in the time, put in the effort, give when you don't feel like giving. As my mother likes to say, "There's a pony under that manure."

62.

AS far and wide the vernal breeze

Sweet odours waft from blooming trees,

So, too, the grateful savour spreads

To distant lands of virtuous deeds.

Sanskrit.

Translation - Hang tight! The karma wagon is wheeling its way back around to you. I just can't say when it's going to arrive. But trust me, it's coming. Until then, don't grow weary of doing the right thing. More people are watching than you think.

Teacher Appreciation Week rocks! Notes in your boxes, BOGOs at your favorite restaurants, and unexpected gifts/treats are hard to beat. But that week seems to take awfully long to arrive... and disappears just as quickly. Recognition would be nice throughout the year, but sadly, that's not the nature of what we do. Most of the time, it's not until years later, when you're a little slower and grayer, do the kids return wiser, bigger, and appreciative. Nevertheless, your virtuous deeds travel far beyond you, them, and likely your school. Be grateful you do and will have such an impact.

IN this world, however little happiness may have been our portion, yet have we no desire to die. Whether he can speak of life as cheerful and delicate, or as full of pain, anxiety, and sorrow, never yet have I seen one who wished to die.

Firdausī.

Translation - Life is precious. Never assume someone's life is worthless just because *you* think so. They have a lot of life left in them, and so do you.

'You're just a teacher', some will say. Often times, we are over-looked by society, and even the children we've come to serve. It can get lonely pretty fast and fairly often. Nevertheless, don't give up! Protect your mental health, as that's a very real part of your job. One might even say it's your duty. Don't allow yourself to get so low that you are unable to function for your loved ones and your students. Remember- you don't live at school. Do your best to leave work at school, and then take care of home. Home and school are very different places, for very good reasons.

MEN say that everyone is naturally a lover of himself, and that it is right that it should be so. This is a mistake; for in fact the cause of all the blunders committed by man arises from this excessive self-love. For the lover is blinded by the object loved, so that he passes a wrong judgment upon what is just, good, and beautiful, thinking that he ought always to honour what belongs to himself, in preference to truth. For he who intends to be a great man ought to love neither himself nor his own things, but only what is just, whether it happens to be done by himself or by another.

Plato.

Translation - Step back from a situation to observe all the angles. We operate under implicit biases that can cause us to play favorites and interfere with impartiality, especially dangerous where justice is concerned. Your job is to be just, and that starts with looking in the mirror before looking at your students.

No matter how you might feel, you are not bigger than your students. While you may be physically larger (or possibly smaller) the truth is you are equal to them—not in maturity, age, or life experience but as human beings. Try not to think so highly of your position, but more on your proximity to what's right. Enter each day knowing that justice should be your aim, whether it's enacted by you, another student, a parent, or an administrator. Honor the truth. Place it right up there with a child's safety.

65.

PURPOSE without power is mere weakness and deception; and power without purpose is mere fatuity.

Sa'dī.

Translation - You need strength to rule a classroom and to run a school. But power and not having direction will run a ship aground just as quickly. Stop teaching by the seat of your pants, and stop letting students dictate the effectiveness of your agenda. Lead with power and direction!

Seek ways to empower yourself and your students. Entering each day purposefully will guide your actions — and reactions — throughout the day, and will very likely inspire students to adopt your attitude towards challenging situations. Teachers are definitely limited in what they can say and do in the classroom, however, the master teacher must think outside the box in terms of instruction, discipline, and leadership. What can you do or who can you call on to help realize your vision? Nothing is more fatal to a student's future than a teacher who has the authority and expertise to influence them, but cannot due to a lack of goals or preparation.

Additional Content

In an effort to publish a paperback copy for those who still enjoy 'the feel of a book,' I ran across a small obstacle—Amazon requires at least 100 pages to print lettering on the book's spine. Whoops! So, making lemonade out of lemons, I've decided to republish content from my articles on Medium. Quick thinking, right?! And there you have it, two articles for your viewing pleasure…courtesy of Amazon KDP.

Update: Spine was still too small, and with the added formatting it's once again short of 100 pages. Haha, so much for that! Enjoy the add-ons anyway :)

We All Have Powers...but What Is Your Superpower?

TURNING YOUR POTENTIAL INTO EXPLOSIVE PERSONAL AND FINANCIAL GROWTH BY COMBINING YOUR TALENTS!

Jul 27 · 5 min read

At some point in your life you've asked yourself, "What are my strengths?" or "What am I good at?" — easy enough to ask but pretty hard to answer. Whether it was deciding what to study in undergrad or what kind of business to start, determining your talents was likely a key ingredient to that endeavor's success...and to your personal happiness. Nevertheless, it's hard to know what that skill is and even harder to know what to do with it.

Short Story

I've never really been gifted. In third grade, I struggled with reading and consequently suffered bad marks in almost all of my classes. I could read the words perfectly but comprehension was poor. Worst of all? I didn't know how to 'fix' my deficiency. So, my teacher set a parent-teacher conference to discuss my academic options. In short, we were recommended remedial classes across the board and possibly being held back a grade.

Well, my mother wasn't having any of that! She politely refused my teacher's suggestion and left tight-lipped, not looking down at me once. When we got in the car, she drove to a big-box bookstore and purchased around 20 books on various subjects — but mostly reading. I suspected then that that would be my life over the next six months...and it was.

Friends knocked on my door almost every afternoon and received a familiar reply almost every time.

"Can Nick come out and play?"

"Tell your friends no, Nicholas," my mom would say, standing right next to me at the door.

"Sorry, I have homework," I'd respond, on the brink of tears, watching the sun dance behind them.

"Okay," they'd relent…or sometimes shoot one final shot.

"Well, what about tomorrow?"

"We'll see about tomorrow when it gets here," shutting the door before her final words escaped.

I knew what that meant. That meant *nope*.

Long story short — and here's the clincher — I learned something from that experience. When I finally began to comprehend what I was reading, I discovered I had a knack for applying what I understood more effectively and expeditiously than most. What's more, I found the information useful and decided to combine my intense drive — that was formerly only for video games and sports — with the realm of self-help material.

And that was my first superpower: Drive + Application.

Fast forward, I am now a prolific reader and writer…and an English teacher! Who would've guessed!? And since then, I've discovered, developed, and honed a few more superpowers. For instance, my ability to simplify complex matters and articulate them with charisma and precision has resulted in a rewarding teaching career — taking me all over the globe and inside some of the best institutions of learning in the world — and a budding, freelance writing gig! Needless to say, discovering your superpower is a worthwhile (and fun) endeavor! And I want to assist you in that.

So, let's uncover your talents!

Unearthing Your Abilities in 5 Steps

Past Success — One way to discover your latent powers is to think about what skills or personality traits have helped you find success in your personal life, career, or schooling. Can you put together some commonalities? Perhaps you've always been able to see big-picture, or you've always had an eye for details.

Au Naturale — What have you always been good at? Ask your friends and family. What areas or activities do you find that just click, or goals you've reached without putting in much effort? Make a list.

Ask others — The power of social media makes this step easy. Post a status on Facebook or Instagram and simply ask your friends what they perceive your talents to be. If that's uncomfortable, give them a call. Or pull a coworker to the side. If you seem honest about your inquiry, they'll likely respond in kind.

Try new things — I grew up playing soccer, basketball, football, and tennis. Never imagined that one day I would chase a loose ball down the court and win the attention of my high school track coach. He asked me to join the team and I did... and on the first day of practice I puked on his shoes. However, three years later I would receive numerous track scholarships. Never know where your talents lie!

Study your hobbies — What do you do for fun? Look for patterns across your hobbies. Maybe it's competition you seek, or building structures, or strategizing that makes you giddy. What activities put you in a state of flow — where time flies or you can perform that activity all day and without financial gain?

Look over these five steps again. Hopefully you wrote down a few things. Now, combine them! Maybe your love of riddles and attention to detail could turn you into an ace detective; maybe your physical strength and will-to-win could result in a stellar athletic or coaching career; maybe you have mountains of charisma, a way with words, and motivational speaking is calling your name. Go for it! Don't be afraid to try.

We all have powers. The key to your success is leveraging your powers by combining them to form a superpower. Superpowers earn the big bucks, change lives, and make the world a better place. Almost every successful person has blended their talents to become a shooting star. Beauty + Singing ability; Analytical mind + A love of sport; Charisma + Acting ability.

At the very least, hard-work is a power. Not many people have that. Trust me, it counts as a power. If you combine a solid work-ethic with just one other legitimate skill in your possession, that resulting force will carry you towards a righteous and prosperous future.

I wish you well.

I Can't Become a Motivational Speaker Because I'm Not Successful

ACCORDING TO ONE OF MY STUDENTS-AND I'M HIS FAVORITE TEACHER-MOTIVATIONAL SPEAKING IS ONLY FOR THE RICH AND SUCCESSFUL. AND I'M NOT THAT.

Jul 31 · 6 min read

"But how can you be motivational speaker, Mr. Landers…if you are not successful?"

Not going to lie, that was tough to hear, given that the words were from a student I'd known for three years and who was now 20 years old. To make matters worse, I was his favorite teacher of any school year. And so I sat there quietly, listening to his gruff but youthful voice traveling through my telephone speaker-we are talking on WhatsApp.

"I mean, don't get me wrong, you are very nice teacher but why will people listen to you?"

He really sounded perplexed, and in a way, so was I. Obviously, I was not successful to him. Despite my education, my teaching prowess, and my character…it appeared I needed money to help others define and find their own measure of success. What a wallop!

And so I sat there, not saying anything but instead thinking, thinking about what to say next. Despite our cultural differences - he is from Romania and I am from the United States - he did have a point. Who would want to learn from someone who had nothing to show for it? I thought about my lean bank account, my 'luxurious' Banana Republic shirts, and my cherished teaching certificate. I thought about my trophies as an athlete and a coach, my travels around the world, and the languages I speak. I thought on the names of thousands of students I've encountered in my decade of teaching and wondered if I'd helped any at all…and then I cleared my voice.

Setting the Stage

"Iacob, I'm not sure how to answer that," I uttered, taking my time. "Certainly, money would help a great deal in convincing others of my value. Even you think so -

"Mr. Landers, I'm sorry."

"No, no, it's okay. There's some truth to that. I think people need to see something before they believe something. But consider this; haven't I been of help to you?"

"Yeah, yeah. Definitely. You are my favorite teacher. Of course, Mr. Landers. You know this."

"I think then that motivational speaking is not about being an example of success but more about helping others to discover, believe in, and unleash the potential they didn't know they had. And those latent powers that are released will hopefully guide them to whatever their idea of success is. Does that make sense?"

His voice sounded more hopeful now and the tiniest bit contrite, "Yes, you're right, Mr. Landers. You are always right. Yes, yes, maybe you can become motivational speaker."

"Thanks, Iacob -

"It's just that, how can you start this? How do you just have nothing and go do something? Do you know some people? What will you talk about?"

It makes complete sense that you should know something about what you plan to pursue - especially when it's a career change! But I didn't have anything too specific in mind. So, I answered what I could.

"Do I know people, like people who are public speakers, or people who can help me get started?"

"Both!"

"Well, I know one motivational speaker. He's a confidence coach."
"What is his name?"

"His name?"

"Yes, I want to see if he's famous."

I laughed a little. Suppose I would've asked the same thing if the roles were reversed.

"Stan Pearson II. Look him up," I capitulated.

"Okay, thank you. Now, do you know people who can make this happen for you?"

It sounded awkward, the tail end of his sentence, make this happen for you. I wasn't really looking for anyone to make something happen for me, mostly because I intended - and intend - to make it happen myself. So I responded to that instead.
"Listen, Iacob, no one is going to make this happen for me. They don't even know me yet. And the ones who do? I think you'll find as you get older that a lot of people are just plain

busy" - I didn't want to say disinterested but I believe he connected the dots.

"I see," he exhaled loudly into the receiver. Some seconds of silence passed. "And so if you will not teach about money-making money-then what?"

"Since you ask, and since we're on the topic...I'll talk about *success*."

He laughed heartily. It was the kind of laugh that made me want to laugh, too, and so I did.

"I see what you are doing, Mr. Landers. Okay, okay, tell me about success."

Teaching from the Heart: The World Is Your Oyster

"Consider this my first speech then. Ready?"

"Yes, I'm listening. This better be good if you are going to do this profession-professionally."

"Alright, alright, I get it. Here we go. Earlier, you told me I was not successful, yes?"

"Ugghh. Please don't remind me. But yes, I say this."

"And it was about money, right?"

"Mr. Landers, what are you doing? Are you trying to make me feel bad?"

"I'm just asking questions."

"Yes, yes. Okay. I did. God! This is the worst motivational speech of my life," he fussed.

"It's not that damn bad," I returned.

"Mr. Landers! You curse? I have never heard you curse."

"Anywayyyy, I want to separate you from such a toxic notion, that money equals success. So, another question -

"Jesus Christ!"

Ignoring his protest, "Would you consider a lottery winner a success?"

"No, of course not."
"Why not?"

"Because they didn't do anything for the money."

"Precisely. That is, if we're talking about money. But what about the action?"

"What action?"

"They purchased a ticket."

"Yes, and they were lucky! That's it."
"A ticket costs money, Iacob. They had to spend money to make money. They had to take on risk."

"So they took a risk. So what? They're going to tell people about taking risks?"

"Precisely."

"So they will tell others about taking risks…because they won money in a game?"

"Couldn't someone use that story to teach others about taking risks, or consequences of not taking risks."

"I see what you are doing, Mr. Landers. You are saying we all have stories and can teach people."

"Partially."

"What is partially?"

"It means halfway."

"So what is the other half?"

"I want you to understand that success is more than money; it's about whatever you want it to be, though I believe the best form of success is an outcome or station that allows you to serve others, or help them share in your prosperity. Overcoming obstacles is a form of success; Enduring trials is a form of success; believing in yourself is a form of success. All of these things are hard to do."

"Hmm, I agree."

"Storytelling is the oldest form of learning and teaching, and I believe if I can learn how to tell stories and combine that skill with my experiences, I can become a motivational speaker. Because I am the success story. Me. And I don't need money to teach you that you are worth something. Got it?"

"Mr. Landers," the airwaves grew still, "I think you will make great motivational speaker."

www.ingramcontent.com/pod-product-compliance
Lightning Source LLC
Chambersburg PA
CBHW072108280526
45788CB00006B/2445